FOND DU LAC PUBLIC LIBRARY

Monkeys WITHDRAWN

By Julie Guidone

Reading Consultant: Susan Nations, M.Ed.,
author/literacy coach/consultant in literacy development

WEEKLY READER®
PUBLISHING

Please visit our web site at **www.garethstevens.com**.
For a free catalog describing our list of high-quality books,
call 1-800-542-2595 (USA) or 1-800-387-3178 (Canada).
Our fax: 1-877-542-2596

Library of Congress Cataloging-in-Publication Data

Guidone, Julie.
      Monkeys / by Julie Guidone ; reading consultant, Susan Nations.
          p. cm. — (Animals that live in the rain forest)
      Includes bibliographical references and index.
      ISBN-10: 1-4339-0024-6   ISBN-13: 978-1-4339-0024-2 (lib. bdg.)
      ISBN-10: 1-4339-0106-4   ISBN-13: 978-1-4339-0106-5 (softcover)
      1. Monkeys—Juvenile literature. I. Title.
  QL737.P9G88   2009
  599.8-dc22   2008030395

This edition first published in 2009 by
Weekly Reader® Books
An Imprint of Gareth Stevens Publishing
1 Reader's Digest Road
Pleasantville, NY 10570-7000 USA

Executive Managing Editor: Lisa M. Herrington
Senior Editor: Barbara Bakowski
Creative Director: Lisa Donovan
Designers: Michelle Castro, Alexandria Davis
Photo Researcher: Diane Laska-Swanke
Publisher: Keith Garton

Photo Credits: Cover © Arctic Images/Getty Images; pp. 1, 15 © SA Team/Foto Natura/Minden
Pictures; pp. 5, 19 © Luciano Candisani/Minden Pictures; p. 7 © Pete Oxford/naturepl.com; p. 9
© Arco Images GmbH/Alamy; p. 11 © Theo Allofs/Minden Pictures; p. 13 © Juniors Bildarchiv/Alamy;
pp. 17, 21 © Nick Gordon/naturepl.com

Printed in the United States of America

1 2 3 4 5 6 7 8 9 10 09 08

Table of Contents

Boldface words appear in the glossary.

At Home in the Trees

A **rain forest** is a warm, wet place. Many plants and animals live in the thick woods.

**golden lion
tamarin monkey**

5

Monkeys live in the rain forests of Central and South America. They spend most of their time in the trees.

capuchin
(kuh-PYOO-shun)
monkeys

Monkeys use their long arms to climb through trees. Strong tails also help them hold on to branches.

tail

arms

9

Making Some Noise

The howler monkey is one of the loudest animals on Earth. A bone in the monkey's throat helps the animal make a noisy **call**.

howler
monkey

In the morning, these monkeys howl before they eat. At night, they howl before they go to sleep. A group of howler monkeys can be heard miles away!

female

male

13

The monkeys also make noise when **predators** are near. Predators kill other animals for food. A baby howler monkey rides on its mother's body to stay safe.

Hanging Around

The spider monkey lives high in the treetops. The tops of most trees make up the rain forest **canopy**. When this monkey hangs from its long tail, it looks like a spider!

spider monkey

tail

17

A spider monkey has long, thin arms. The monkey uses its arms and tail to swing quickly from tree to tree.

A strong tail comes in handy at mealtime! The spider monkey uses its tail to hang from a branch. Its hands are free to grab fruit, flowers, and nuts to eat.

fruit

Glossary

call: the typical cry or sound of an animal

canopy: the top layer of a rain forest

predators: animals that kill and eat other animals

rain forest: a warm, rainy woodland with many types of plants and animals

For More Information

Books

Howler Monkeys. Animals of the Rain Forest (series). Sandra Donovan (Raintree, 2003)

Little Monkey Lost. Keith DuQuette (G.P. Putnam's Sons, 2007)

Web Sites

National Geographic News: Howler Monkeys— World's Loudest Animals?
news.nationalgeographic.com/news/2006/09/ 060927-monkey-video.html
Watch and listen to noisy howler monkeys.

PBS: Journey Into Amazonia
www.pbs.org/journeyintoamazonia/explorer.html
Play Amazon Explorer! Visit the rain forest canopy to learn about howler monkeys and other treetop animals.

Index

About the Author

Julie Guidone has taught kindergarten and first and second grades in Madison, Connecticut, and Fayetteville, New York. She loves to take her students on field trips to the zoo to learn about all kinds of animals! She lives in Syracuse, New York, with her husband, Chris, and her son, Anthony.